A management game for social services

Anthony S Hall and Jimmy Algie

o६।३ঀ

Published for the
National Institute for Social Work
by the
Bedford Square Press of the
National Council of Social Service
26 Bedford Square London WC 1

ISBN 0 7199 0887 6

Distributed by Research Publications Services
Victoria Hall East Greenwich London SE10 0RF

Design and typography by NCSS Publications Department
Printed in England by Ditchling Press Ltd Ditchling Sussex

Contents

Introduction

By evoking and exploiting students' own resources instead of pouring in factual knowledge, Homer Lane, A S Neill, David Wills and their followers carried through the revolution of progressive education.[1] Using such methods the teacher becomes a non-directive enabler. Students learn through what they do and discover rather than from formal chalk-and-talk instruction. This revolution has worked its way through the educational hierarchy. Now it affects even post-experience and post-professional training where extensive experience of managers and pro-fessionals contributes as much knowledge in educational situations as any trainer has to offer.

A number of research studies have demonstrated the severe limitations of lectures as a teaching method.[2] Only a small proportion of presented material is 'heard': an even smaller proportion is retained, let alone applied. Group discussions are more participative in that all group members work together towards certain common objectives. Small groups help facilitate attitude-changes, foster critical analysis, unravel confusions in language and concept, ensure participants communicate as well as invite ideas and information. But however vividly examples are drawn from the group members' practical experience, discussions remain ineffably theoretical. They become divorced from concrete processes and real constraints of work situations. Problems of applying new learning to daily work increase. Systematic ordering of knowledge may give place to random, haphazard treatment of material—one fault from which efficient lectures do not suffer.

Simulation-gaming allows the process of participative training to be taken much further. A stronger relationship is established with daily work processes and real-life decision-making. By playing through a simulation game, decision-makers can test alternative courses of action, make mistakes and learn from them, systematically plan what to do in advance, and apply their knowledge and experience in a concrete way.

This pamphlet describes a work game which the authors developed at the National Institute for Social Work[3]. Though intended primarily as a training and decision-making device for use by senior and middle manage-ment personnel in social service departments, it is capable of modification for use by a variety of planning groups.

Social services resource allocation game

The game focuses on the interplay between rational decision-making and political bargaining which takes place when allocating scarce resources within a local authority social services department. It comprises a series of rounds, each representing a complete financial year in the life of one such agency. Eight role-players, representing key decision-makers, negotiate and bargain for policies which they believe the agency should follow. Outcomes of discussions and negotiations are observed by the *System*, four people who represent all aspects of the agency system not otherwise simulated. They make periodic pronouncements as to how agency policy seems to be evolving and on the effect of this on the influence each role-player may exert in subsequent rounds. After several rounds, the experience of the game is discussed in an extensive de-briefing session which centres on strategies and tactics employed, the decision-making processes, and the reality reflected in the simulation. Modifications and additions can be made to the game to highlight aspects of the department's work or environment which players feel are particularly important and need to be emphasised.

Game versus reality

In real-life decision-making, we may postulate the following general situation. Decision-makers decide what objectives they wish to pursue, what additional resources they require, how they will gain sanctions for them, and what allocations of resources will achieve the desired policies. Since total departmental resources are limited, any policy proposed by one participant is limited by policies advocated by others. Staff have to contend with a complex environment while forced to compete with other subsectional interests for scarce resources. They find they are compelled to use not only rational argument but other less rational methods of exerting influence, such as pressurising, in order to make their fullest contribution to the organisation's work. Their actions are based on what they think is best for the community served by the organisation, what they would like the section they represent to achieve, and their own personal objectives.

Conflicts result. Their outcomes determine what contribution players are able to make, hence their power to implement favoured policies and achieve personal objectives such as promotion, increased job-security, popularity. Chance and uncontrollable elements play a part, sometimes facilitating their efforts, sometimes hindering them. Fortune may be with them or against them. At all times decision-makers have to observe, analyse and infer the nature of the evolving organisational situation in the light of ongoing events—how the system's mechanism functions as well as

6

how the internal politics are proceeding. This is a somewhat different analysis to that which is concerned with systematic evaluation of the impact of various services on community problems, but one which forms no less a part in achieving effective results.

The game's mechanics are designed to simulate as simply as possible the elements of this real-life situation. Players, it is hoped, acquire a simulated experience of this reality. In analysing their behaviour during the game and in the concluding de-briefing, they understand more clearly how to act effectively in future in respect of political aspects of decision-making and how to work with constraints imposed by the system or context in which they operate. How far the game simulates reality in the last resort depends on participants' personal assumptions about the nature of reality.

Essential elements

Pairs and groups of role-players enter a series of discussions, conflicts and coalitions to arrive at departmental policies and decisions. The *System* periodically reports on how players' actions influence the changing social service system they are managing. Scoreboards are constantly updated, providing a running commentary on the state of play.

The action takes place within a simulated social service department. Sometimes players make whatever assumptions they please about the setting, provided these are specified. At other times, a detailed description and balance-sheet of a fictional department is presented in advance with deliberate deficiencies in its range of provision. Providing a minimal outline of the organisation enables players to concentrate on what impact they themselves might make on the changing nature of the organisation and its interaction with the community.

Participants are divided into two main groups—players, that is decision-makers, and members of the *System*. Players are allocated between eight decision-making or management roles.[4] Using the game for training social services managers, the roles are usually defined as follows: director, social services department; assistant director, fieldwork services; assistant director, residential care; assistant director, planning and research; assistant director, domiciliary and day care; chief administrative officer; training officer; president, consumers association. In formulating agency policies, each role-player represents the interests of his own section or area of responsibility.

The eight roles refer to an expected or characteristic pattern of decision-making based on a combination of sectional interests and personal objectives. They do not necessarily refer to any characteristic behaviour patterns. A further dimension may be added by defining a style or manner of behaviour in which particular roles should be performed. Thus, the game may be played with an authoritarian director, a militant consumer

7

representative, a bureaucratic administrative officer concerned primarily with curtailing expenditure, a permissive fieldwork services director and so on. Alternatively players fill their roles as nearly as possible as they would in reality. However it is important to note that the management group of a social service department is not itself being simulated, but the agency processes with which these role-players are concerned.

Members of the *System* each represent particular features of the total system within which the role-players operate. Their deliberations on changes in the system are basic to the game. Using the relationships built into the model, the *System* processes decisions so as to produce a series of reports on the outcome of players' activities during each round. Every round simulates a specific time period, usually a financial year. In this way many years of operations may be covered in a single day. A co-ordinator ensures that the mechanics run smoothly, and two scorers continuously revising the scoreboards which indicate the state of play. An observer comments to role-players on the interactions and group dynamics manifested during play.

Influence

Decision-makers pursue desired policy objectives by using the influence[5] they wield in the department. In the simulation, role-players begin with varying amounts of influence at their disposal. The influence each player can command is tangibly registered by the number of pegs he holds for voting on items of policy as they arise. As the game progresses, each player's influence fluctuates depending on how far he is influential in guiding overall agency policy. If a player succeeds in representing his own interests during voting, his influence (ie his number of pegs) increases. If he fails to represent his interests, and those of his section, his influence (number of pegs) decreases.

Players use their influence to further their policy objectives. Performance during the game is evaluated not in terms of how much influence players hold during play, but by how far each player's policy objectives have been fulfilled or, at least, furthered. These objectives are specified before gaming starts.

Voting

Role-players throughout decide what they would like to see happen in the department and use their influence accordingly by voting on agenda items as they arise round by round. Every role-player has his own voting board and a number of influence pegs. He distributes his influence by

Figure 1 *(see page* 8)

ROLE-PLAYERS VOTING BOARD

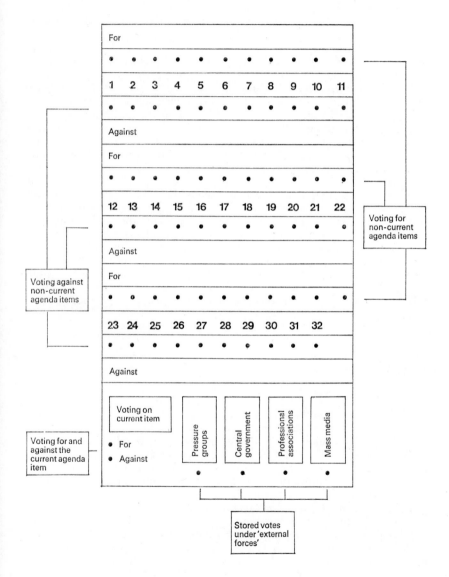

slotting his pegs into chosen holes on the peg-board which record his votes. If he so chooses, a player may pile all his pegs into only one hole rather than disperse them over the board. He can in other words, attempt to influence one thing decisively or, at the other extreme, endeavour to play a role in everything, thereby probably never achieving anything fully. Voting is crucial to the game's dynamics. Players fare well or ill depending on how they use their votes.

Votes are cast in one of five ways. Players may vote *for* or *against* the current agenda item up for discussion during that round. Alternatively they may vote *for* or *against* any other agenda item yet to come up for discussion. This has the effect of promoting or demoting non-current agenda items and influences their future likelihood of becoming part of departmental policy. The fifth voting possibility is to *store* influence under one of the 'external forces'. This simulates the tapping of the good will of parties outside the department in furthering intra-departmental objectives. Stored influence is retrieved later in the game to support or oppose any item about which the player has strong convictions. A player uses it when his favoured item comes to be put to the vote. However, stored influence increases or decreases depending on how external forces react to the direction departmental policies are taking.

Players choose their voting strategy and vote according to their interests, but in the light of constraints like a limited budget, the demands of fellow-players for reciprocity in bargaining, the current departmental situation, and so on. The voting process represents the decision-making procedure of the department on matters of policy. The voting outcome on each issue, therefore, represents not only acceptance or rejection of a particular agenda item, but also the introduction of a specific direction in departmental policy. Thus for example, if players pass an agenda item to establish car allowances for home helps at an annual cost of £2,000, this begins to suggest the development of a policy of extending community services.

Agenda items

The central feature of the game is agenda items (see figure 2 page 15). A set of these is included in the game materials section (see Appendix III, page 38). The specific items included on the agenda reflect generalised issues covering the whole spectrum of different needs within the social services. They represent a wide range of alternative policies between which choices must be made. For example, decisions have to be made whether to develop community care services (item 10) or extend and improve residential provisions (item 11), or what balance to achieve between them and at what cost. Similarly, how far should preventive work be developed (item 15) as opposed to improving social casualty services (item 30) how far services should cater for a heterogeneous range of clientele (item 28) or be selectively directed at priority areas of special need (item 2).

There is no order of agenda issues laid down in advance of the game. However, each issue has a prior degree of likelihood of arising, and therefore of being passed, based on an assessment of the issue's significance, precedent, tradition and fashion. This likelihood is expressed in terms of pegs pre-cast in favour of or against agenda items. Each agenda item is rated by the amount of influence it commands at any one time within the agency system. This is graded on a points scale (see figure 2, page 15). The rating of each item is revised at the end of every round on the basis of voting on the item under discussion. After all, in reality we do find that certain issues are automatically more favourably received than others, being peculiarly fitted to the organisational culture.

At the start of each round, one agenda item is selected for discussion and voting. For this purpose a bag of randomly-assorted balls is introduced to represent the element of chance in organisational operations. In this bag, thirty-two numbered balls represent each of the agenda items. A further thirty-two balls are blank. If a numbered ball is withdrawn, tombola-style, from the bag, then the corresponding item comes up for discussion and voting. When a blank is drawn, the item with the greatest amount of existing influence is selected.

There is a fifty-fifty chance of random, uncontrolled or unpredictable factors altering the course of the planning process against players' intentions by a numbered ball being selected, thus temporarily disturbing the pattern of conscious decisions players have taken. We may vary this probability according to how far chance is thought in practice to influence events in social service departments, or how far players need more experience in responding to unpredictable occurrences. This process represents not only the element of randomness in life, but also the effect of things handled elsewhere in the local authority which lie outside the view of those participating in the game, and the existence of constraints originating elsewhere.

The play

The game comprises a series of rounds. For each round, an agenda item is selected from the agenda list. Role-players discuss the selected issue in the context of desired agency policy, other items already passed and those elsewhere on the agenda, budgetary allowances (fixed at 33 per cent of the total annual cost of implementing the entire agenda) and other factors entering the decision-making process. Each round lasts about twenty minutes. This period enables players to gain support from others and form alliances; to assess likely voting on this and other items; to evaluate the state of play; to argue merits and demerits of issues involved. Through this process, players develop a variety of liaisons and strategies to ensure the passing or failing of the agenda item under discussion, and likelihood of other items reaching the discussion table. While the passing or failing of the current agenda item is crucial in that this will be taken by the *System* as indicative of trends in organisational policy, voting on non-current agenda items can promote other items in the agenda to favourable positions, thus increasing the possibility of their coming up for discussion.

Given these complexities, each player must take into account a wide range of variables when deciding how to vote or in what direction to influence others' voting. This necessitates a deep understanding of social policy implications of items and of the inter-relations between them. Skills in coping with variety and complexity of real-life situations through time are paramount.

At the end of each round the votes for and against the current agenda item, together with the existing degree of influence for that item, determine whether the issue has been passed or rejected. Another step has been taken in deciding the direction of departmental policy, as in the following example:

Example—Round 3

Item 16

Votes *for* item	+20
Votes *against* item	— 5
Total	+15
Existing level of influence for item 16	+10
Therefore, item 16 passed by	+ 25 points

It is clear from this example that had the existing level of influence of agenda item 16 been, say — 20, the item would have failed despite the majority of favourable votes cast by role-players. The overall influence of any one item then may range from + 25 to — 25 points. If players take insufficient account of contributory influences when voting, items may well fail despite majority support, and vice versa. Decisions are by no means always carried on the will of the majority. Once the result of voting on the current agenda item has been calculated, *System* members give their inter-round analyses of the state of play, hence of the agency.

The system

The *System* articulates all those tangible and intangible factors and constraints embedded in the total social service system within which role-players operate which are not predesigned in the simulation model. They calculate the effects of decisions on other parts of the system and of the passing or failing of the agenda item voted on in the previous round.

12

Social systems are organised dynamic assemblages of interacting and complex parts. These parts are functions, services or sections. They cohere to form a system which is greater than the sum of their parts. They exhibit inherent directionality or apparent purpose. Their parts interact in ways which seem to push them steadily towards certain preferred end-states. People participating in the system may have conscious objectives which are opposed to the directions in which the system would move were its mechanics left untouched. Participants involved in the system, therefore, constantly seek to rewrite the programmes by which the system works in order to reorganise or negate the system's inherent constraints. In the game, members of the *System* identify for role-players the inherent directionality of the total social services system being simulated. At the same time, it registers changes in direction by revising the system's operating dynamics as these are affected by players' behaviour. Though the *System* does not evaluate specific behaviour of players—for instance, they do not observe the bargaining processes during rounds— they do monitor the effects of players' decisions by observing changes in departmental policy which result from voting.

Functions of the system

The *System* answers the question: what sort of social service agency is being developed by the sum total of decisions made by the players, round by round? In one sense they represent the nature of the total system in all its inter-related parts. Their work is performed by four members of the group each dealing with a particular aspect which we will now explore.

1 Effects of agenda items

Each major decision affects subsequent decisions. One member of the *System* assesses how the passing or failing of the current agenda item affects each other item on the agenda. Passage or failure of an item, it is assumed, reflects departmental policy. Other items associated with this policy increase or decrease in their influence accordingly. The influence rating is reassessed for each item in the light of the most recent round of voting. (See example, page 15.)

The passing or rejection of one item affects the likelihood of other items coming forward (ie its influence rating) in one of two ways. First, an item which is passed may require additional resources to be invested in it in order to maximise the value of its implementation. Other items on the agenda which incorporate these necessary resources, therefore, have an increased likelihood of coming forward for discussion. For example, if item 2 is passed, this suggests that the department is following a policy of positive discrimination in favour of key priority areas of need. Such a policy is likely to depend on the availability of trained community workers (item 15) rather than upon the employment of psychodynamically oriented caseworkers (item 25). As a result item 15 becomes highly desirable and its influence on the agenda increases accordingly. Item 25, on the other hand, becomes immediately less relevant in the context of current departmental planning, and its influence rating wanes. Conversely, if item 2 is rejected, this implies that a positive discrimination policy will not be adopted. In this situation, item 25, related to training skilled caseworkers, is more likely to come forward as representing an alternative training policy development, while item 15, community work training, becomes less likely, unless some other policy is established which requires an increase in community work skills. In this way, the game simulates the dynamic properties of any social service system in which decisions are seen to have ramifying and reverberating effects (often unintended) on all other operations.

There is a second major way in which the passage or failure of an item influences the rating of other items by the *System*. If an item is passed authorising expenditure of resources on one particular area of the agency's activities, key decision-makers may be less likely to pass any further expenditure in the same area of activity. For example, it could be argued that in passing item 3 we improve the administrative backing of the social work services. Further expenditure in the same direction, as suggested in item 4, might be seen as superfluous in the context of the whole system, at least until sufficient time had elapsed for the relevance of improved administrative backing to reassert itself. Passing item 3 would in this case lead to a down rating of item 4 (and vice versa should the occasion arise).

In deciding how the passage or failure of one item consequentially affects the others, the *System* explores all possible inter-relationships between different items. Many of the items may not directly, of themselves, inter-relate. They have a mutual impact only in so far as they are parts of the same social services system and therefore constitute claims on the same pool of scarce resources. The act of balancing one need against another, though painful and perhaps involving uncertain assumptions for which we need more evidence, is a common agency problem. Managers have to take action even where relevant evidence is lacking.

The *System* bases its deliberations and assessments not only on the policy implications of the current agenda item but, as the game progresses, on the composite appearance of the items passed. Were item 15 passed, this would suggest a possible move by the department in the direction of community care. In the next round, were item 32 also passed, or were item 10 rejected, this would suggest that some form of balanced overall policy was being devised. If, on the other hand, item 32 was rejected or item 10 passed, this might indicate an increasing agency commitment to community care. In this latter case, the result would be a further marking down of the non-community based items elsewhere in the agenda.

For each round, therefore, one item is chosen, discussed, voted on and is (say) passed. A member of the *System* is responsible for assessing the current influence rating of every other agenda item as a result of this vote. At the end of the round he summarises for role-players the assumptions on which his decisions were based, and announces his revised ratings in detail. These are registered on the *agenda items* score-board.

Finally, role-players' votes cast during the previous round on non-current items are incorporated as in the following example:

Example—Round 3

Assume that during the round, item 14 was the current agenda item discussed and passed. At the end of the round revised ratings for non-current items are announced.

Level of influence for item 17 at the start of round 3 = 15.

Revised rating as announced by the *System* as a result of the passage of item 14 = + 20.

Add additional influence for the item representing votes cast by role-players for item 17 during round 3 = +5.

Therefore the level of influence for item 17 during round 4 will be +25.

Figure 2

AGENDA ITEMS BOARD

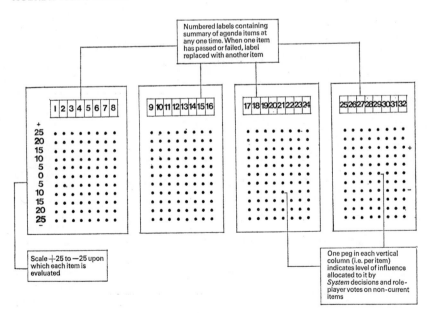

15

By voting on non-current items, players can to some extent counteract or reinforce *System* decisions. Their power in this respect is limited. They cannot radically reverse the direction in which the system is moving (as embodied in the *System's* decisions) without highly co-ordinated corporate activities. A major lesson of the game is the need for corporate rather than competing planning and control by decision-makers.

2 Player influences

Decision-makers' influence varies through time. A second member of the *System* assesses the effects of the passage or failure of the current agenda item on each role-player's level of influence in a similar way to that used in analysing probable effects on other agenda items. The *player influence board* (figure 3) records how the influence of each role-player varies as the game proceeds. The *System* describes at the end of each round the principles on which these changes were calculated. For example, the *System* may suggest that the assistant director, residential care is losing influence because of the department's drift in policy towards a greater emphasis on community care.

Figure 3

PLAYER INFLUENCE BOARD

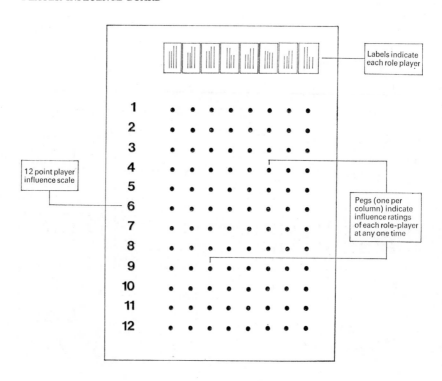

16

Each player's influence rating is indicated on a 12 point scale. The number of voting pegs provided for each player in the next round is calculated as twice the number of points of influence shown on this scale.

3 External influences

Decisions have effects outside the department. With this in mind, a third member of the *System* examines the effect of the passing or failing of agenda items on four external bodies—the mass media, pressure groups, central government, and professional associations. Again, each begins the game with a prior degree of influence. The *System* assesses progressive changes in this influence. This affects the extent to which players' stored influence accumulates or dissipates (see *Voting*, page 10). Stored pegs are augmented or diminished according to the favourable or unfavourable reactions of the bodies under which they are stored, for example, to trends in departmental policy. A player anticipates a favourable reaction from the central government if the current agenda item is passed. He gets the item through by persuading others to vote for it. When voting, he invests his own influence (as registered by his pegs) under central government. If the item was passed, and he successfully predicted the system's dynamics, the amount of his stored influence with central government would increase proportionately. He can withdraw this stored influence at any time to use it for voting in the normal way. Conversely, players may miscalculate the voting. The items may be rejected. He may misinterpret the central government's reaction. If so, the influence he invested under central government is reduced. How often do real-life managers feel similar frustrations having invested time and energy in cultivating inter-organisational links with an external agency only to find that their efforts have been frustrated by things happening elsewhere? Variations in the reactions of external influence are recorded by the relevant member of the *System* on a 10 point scale.

4 Overall structural influences

Major decisions affect the overall agency and community situation. To simulate this effect, one member of the *System* summarises the overall state of the departmental system at the end of each round, pointing up significant trends, possible consequences of over-playing or ignoring particular policies, and so on.

System members explain their judgements to assembled players. Their word is final. No-one is allowed to question these judgements. All that is required of the *System* is that its members' assessments are reasonably consistent, coherent, or consistently inconsistent according to some basic set of axioms. Such consistency is necessary to enable players to deduce the underlying assumptions on which the *System* bases its comments. Only when players can assess the likely effects these will have on the mechanics of the game and, therefore, come to understand something about how the total system operates can they modify their own actions accordingly to effect desired changes and thus influence the state of play and the policies developed and implemented by the agency.

Scoreboards

The boards involved in the game include:

Player voting boards (figure 1)
These boards record each role-player's distribution of influence (ie pegs) during the current round. The distribution will cover influence cast for or against the current agenda item, influence cast for or against non-current agenda items, and influence stored with external forces for future records.

Agenda issues board (figure 2)
This board records the influence of each current issue within the department.

Player influence board (figure 3)
This board records the current influence of each game role-player within the department.

External influence board
This board records the reaction of external forces to agency decisions on a 10 point scale.

De-briefing

Before the game, each player privately records (see *Essential game materials IV*, page 27) the policies which he would like the agency to pursue during the course of the game. He assesses the degree of priority he attached to each agenda item and the strategy he intends using to gain his objectives. At the end of play, each player evaluates his own performance by comparing his initial objectives with the fortunes of his favoured agenda items during the game. Who wins or loses is less important than what players have learnt during play or through retrospective analysis.

The de-briefing session enables everyone to examine their experience, to evaluate their individual performances and that of the group, to criticise the game and the technique, and to discuss the operational processes highlighted in the game.

Some lessons players say they have learnt include:
Recognising the significance of planning in day-to-day work
Improved skill in timing of decisions
How to organise and work with groups
How to decide priorities in developing services and evaluating effectiveness
The vulnerability of the decision-maker

The ease with which resources and influence can be wasted
Negative feelings which can develop if an individual in the group is neglected
Improved decision-making methods
The importance of reaching a dynamic balance between interacting divisions and sections
Structural needs of the agency
Concrete personal experience of what can otherwise only be taught theoretically
The interaction between the aspects of human relations and systematic analysis, both of which are relevant to the work process

Summary

The game comprises a series of rounds during which role-players (representing agency decision-makers) attempt to formulate a departmental policy. At the start of each round an agenda item is selected from a list of agency options. Bargaining continues for about twenty minutes, after which role-players use their 'influence' to vote on whether or not the current item should be incorporated into a final agency policy statement. From the voting results, the four members of the *System* in turn announce the impact of the passing or failing of that agenda item on other elements in the system—namely:

1 other agenda items not yet discussed
2 influence ratings of role-players
3 the reaction of external forces and
4 the state of the total agency system

Scoreboards are updated to incorporate the *System's* pronouncements and votes cast, and the cycle begins again with selection of the next agenda item.

Evaluating game effectiveness

Reviewing the game's effectiveness is a complex business. Here we have attempted to evaluate the game by describing ways in which agencies have reacted to it, its use as a training instrument and its potential use in real-world decision-making. First, since experience of the process itself is claimed as a major benefit, we have completed a scenario which summarises this experience as reported by participants.

The feel of play

Someone adopts a policy of egoistic self-interest. It works for a round or two. The constraints within the system make frustration inevitable. There are always those who try to 'go it alone', seeking to manipulate the whole system on behalf of some personally favoured policy. This succeeds for a short period. Soon it becomes evident that one cannot avoid co-operating with others to achieve even a modest range of objectives. One player gains victory for his own ends in one round only to find, that despite a temporary increase in his formal influence, it has increased his chances of defeat in subsequent play. Stalemate and deadlock between conflicting parties operates for several rounds until it is finally broken up by compromises.

One player begins to regard his collegiate decision-makers as opponents, spending his time bidding for resources against them, matching move and counter-move, taking more account of their reactions than effects on clients. However, he gets his 'come-uppance' as the *System* corrects the disequilibrium of the system, registering the reverberating effect felt by the whole agency if such a policy were to last for long.

The shrewd bargainer, meanwhile, is discovering the nature of the constraints which limit what he can achieve merely through adroit bargaining. Those with power or formal authority discover that command is not of itself sufficient to get decision implemented—that without the support of his staff, the director is not as all-powerful as he might believe himself to be.

One team neglects long-term considerations to capitalise on short-term payoffs, but is brought up short when it runs out of resources and goodwill at a critical point of agency development several rounds later. Another team fails to adapt flexibly to changes as they occur, so fixed is their concentration on longer-term results. They soon learn how far present decisions constrain, limit, guide or dictate future decisions. At one point, participants may be so locked in conflict on behalf of divisional and sectional interests, that they begin to pull the agency apart. This begins to be registered by *System* pronouncements, and slowly participants begin to co-operate in the painful task of reconstructing a demoralised agency.

Suddenly chance intervenes at the least predictable point to turn everything upside down. Just as a clear policy of community care begins to emerge, a 'ministerial circular' is issued requiring considerable improvement in residential provision necessitating radical rethinking about marginal budgetary allocations. As this chance event wreaks havoc, players begin to prepare themselves for some of the more possible contingencies which may occur so as to insure themselves against disasters, placing rough limits on the likelihoods involved.

Genuine co-operation often develops after two or three rounds, those involved perhaps discovering that this is the only way in which change can be effected. Another player gradually gaining ground in respect of his own goals as a result of elaborate and systematic calculations and

20

predictions of events, suddenly finds all his painstaking work overturned by his own political miscalculation. Yet another is still trying to decide what his objectives are.

As the game proceeds, players find themselves increasingly involved in the developing simulation. Arguments and discussions take on a very serious, 'real' appearance. People are by turn angry and aggressive, thoughtful and reflective, perturbed, acquiescent, stubborn, sceptical, jubilant. By lunch-time, some players feel (and look as if) they have undergone a month's experience and learning. Some seem to suffer from 'decision-making fatigue'. Some recognise their mistakes and try to correct them only to find that they have over-reacted and must suffer the consequences. People begin to realise that they cannot get what they want simply by asking for it, nor merely by arguing for it persuasively.

Agency reactions

The game has now been played in various forms by over 200 social and allied service personnel: committee members, directors and assistant directors of social service departments, area directors and fieldworkers. Reactions have been as wide-ranging as the players themselves, from total commitment ('All our training ought to be conducted like this' or 'Social service departments ought to use this to formulate their policies') to complete rejection of the whole gaming concept whatever its purpose. Overall, reactions are favourable.

However favourably or critically received, gaming always generates a seemingly limitless basis for analysis of the nature of political processes, alternative decision-making methods, use of power and influence, ways of effecting change in different situations, constraints felt by public service personnel and how to respond to them, and other fundamental issues of management and policy-making. Though serious in intent, the game is also fun.

Effects as training instrument

The effectiveness of the game as a training method is evaluated by several criteria including participant involvement, enjoyment, individual benefit and group impact on the system. There is undoubtedly more wholehearted participant involvement as compared with other training methods used such as lectures and group discussions. This is demonstrated not only in students' explicit evaluation statements, but also in terms of observable indicators. These include proportions of participants articulating their views, numbers of persons responding directly to others' views, numbers of interactions between participants, numbers of different types of dialogue

21

in which participants are engaged, intensity and persistence with which participants express and press their views, degree of development of participants' arguments in support of their views, degree to which participants are engaged in the gaming process mentally, emotionally and physically. The game scores high on all these counts, even when students believe they have learnt more from a particular lecture or group discussion on an equivalent subject.

The exception to this trend seems to be about one person in every 20 who is 'game-aversive', repelled by games of any kind whether outdoor or indoor sports, card-games or any chance-dependent contest. Aside from this minority group, involvement does not necessarily correlate with enjoyment. In general, student reactions swing violently between the two extremes of felt distaste and positive exhilaration. Few remain lukewarm. Felt distaste may be mollified by working though the emotions engendered during de-briefing. Exhilaration is tempered by sober review of performance. But the emotional associations persist long after the experience. It can be a shattering experience for a real-life director suddenly to find he has lost all his influence in the game, and equally for a role-player who had less formal influence in real-life to find himself all-powerful on one particular issue.

Nor is enjoyment always correlated with success in the game. Those who fare badly sometimes enjoy it enormously, and vice versa. It is also clear that degree of enjoyment and degree of individual benefit derived are not identical. Sometimes in training what we least want is perhaps what we most need, and vice versa. What individual benefits do people derive from the game? We may list the following: greater capacity to envisage a wider variety of problem variables in a situation simultaneously; a longer time span of consideration in predicting probable consequences of action; increased recognition of constraints on implementing desired policies; a larger number of specific ideas on how to overcome these constraints; a more concrete specification of the work entailed in activating such ideas; an enhanced recognition of how day-to-day decisions shape the overall pattern of agency performance; increased recognition of requirements imposed by the overall system on daily decisions. Those who evaluate the game highly on these scores often come away with a completely transformed view of social and agency planning, offering a different range of alternative solutions than would be the case prior to the game. Participants tend not to derive these benefits from the game if their time is consumed in grappling with its mechanics, unable to grasp what the mechanics symbolise, or alternatively if they see the whole exercise in terms of human interaction, treating the whole process as a complicated role-play. The latter group tend to enjoy the game while neither doing very well in it nor deriving other evaluated benefits.

A further significant aspect of performance analysed in the game is the strategy employed by decision-makers in gaining support for their policies. This is evaluated by which alternative set of strategies is employed and how successfully. One strategy might be to choose the course of action, which if successful, would achieve the greatest pay-off, though this risks also the greatest loss. Another might be to choose the course of action, which if it were to fail, would cause the least regret.

Another approach is to evaluate the effectiveness of the participant group as a whole in directing the agency system as modelled in the game. Here it is possible to elicit group views as to their desired objectives for the agency beforehand, comparing these views with the directions in which the modelled agency actually moved as a result of game transactions. In general, we have found that few groups have been able to move the agency system in the directions favoured beforehand. This largely reflects failure to control the multiple variables in the system or to derive a coherent and sufficiently sophisticated policy as a group which satisfies a range of conflicting views and personal motivations of individual members. The only groups who gained unqualified success in this respect were those whose objectives were very modest and where there was large value consensus among members as to what was considered desirable.

In reviewing evaluated results of the game as played amongst diverse social services personnel, an interesting feature emerges. The more determinedly idealistic the group as a whole was, for example supporting a preventive, social advocacy agency, the less attention was paid to the practical mechanics and political bargaining necessary to get decisions carried which would move the agency system in the directions they desired. In one extreme example this resulted in a group being completely unable to make any impact whatsoever on the directions in which the agency system was set to move before the game began. Conversely, the more individuals sought to increase personal power, the greater was the mastery of the practical mechanics and the political processes involved, but the more contradictory and the less coherent was the resulting agency policy. In one instance, this resulted in very powerful control of the agency system by the participant group but enormous uncertainty as to the policy implications of where they were moving the system.

Effects on decision-making

While some agency managers have played the game experimentally to clarify issues involved in allocating scarce agency resources across their services, its use as a primary mechanism for agency policy-making has still to be tested in the field. To evaluate its use in this respect demands that the results of one year's decisions are fed back into the subsequent year's game and that other indicators be used to determine whether the direction of actual agency development corresponds to the directions developed in the system.

In one agency, the managers involved were very clear as to why they had not used the game as a primary policy-making instrument. The state and development of the agency system as evolved through the gaming process became highly explicit to all participants: far more so than normally occurs in course of daily incremental decisions. This led managers to question whether they or their staff found the directions in which they

23

were moving the system (as a result of gaming decisions) were desirable and how they could feasibly reach agreement on changing its direction. This in turn provided the occasion for a series of open-discussion planning meetings in which objectives were to be more clearly defined and agreed. When asked why they did not run these meetings according to the game format, the responses were that they could not handle any additional information such as further rounds of gaming would provide. The game had in any case provided the catalytic process which would enable decisions to be taken in the light of the gaming experience, the fundamental questions of direction and feasibility raised, and the new objectives agreed. They would also wish to mix the decision-making methods, finding it too exhausting to take all decisions on a gaming basis rather than through free-ranging discussion. It was felt that replaying the game periodically using different sets of decisions would accustom them to its use over a period of time, making adjustments easier. The budgetary decisions taken in the open discussions which followed were regarded as easier to make than had previously been the case.

These reactions suggest that the limits of the game as a planning instrument need to be clearly specified, and its use for this purpose phased in with other planning methods. One aspect which seems common to the introduction of new systematic approaches to decision-making is that when managers achieve some satisfaction from short-term pay-offs or from resolving certain specific problems by using the method, there is less incentive to go on to apply the approach comprehensively. This is in line with the tendency to use such approaches to increase understanding of the problem factors involved rather than to use them as methods for deciding how to resolve these problems, the latter resting with discretionary decisions based on individuals' intuition.

Such pilot evaluation methods are suggestive of more rigorous experimental research which might cast light on many existing hypotheses and claims about learning and decision-making effects of simulation games. One problem which has delayed such rigorous evaluation is that a game of this kind already emphasises and sets in motion a self-evaluation process amongst participants, the results of which are themselves fed back in the course of gaming. This means that attempts at external, objective evaluation of results inevitably refer to a highly self-aware set of decision-makers in which the learning process itself may be rapidly transforming the whole system as it is being observed. Although this may be overcome by before-and-after research into attitudes and effects, the measures required are more complex. In relation to training aspects, they will constitute evaluations of participant self-evaluations. In relation to decision-making uses, they are dependent on some progress in evaluating overall agency effectiveness and would probably have to be linked to non-gaming process simulation models.

Conclusion: levels of simulation

The game may be said to operate as a simulation of behaviour and processes at a variety of different levels and in different ways. It provides an interesting basis for discussions about human interpersonal relations and processes of group interaction. It is played in totally different ways by different groups of players. Some prefer to operate as individuals. One set of players, for example, worked almost entirely without consultation or compromise, without forming any major groupings of players until the system was thrown into such disarray with gross overspending and confusion that corporate action was the only answer. Other players form into opposing cliques, battling it out over each issue. Yet others combine as a total group, in corporate management style, and make conjoint decisions by which they hope to influence (or even change the nature of) the system.

Secondly, in some respects the game simulates the actual reality of working within a social service department. The role-players, when in one large group, comprise a not untypical departmental meeting of senior managers. Individual agenda items and more general policy issues discussed in this setting may differ little from actual discussions many have already had in the field.

Third, there are lessons to be learnt from the game itself through its mechanics and complexities. Whether or not the game reproduces or reflects reality in any way at all, it is beyond question that success in playing the game depends on players understanding fully and quickly how the system operates. What will be the effect of putting pegs here? How will the *System* rate this? Is it more important to argue things out or to examine the score-boards in detail? How does the scorer add up the influence in between rounds? Such questions relate to playing the game, not to any simulated reality. Paradoxically the simulation at this level is even more real. Only by understanding how a system works, where built-in power and constraints lie, how they are shifting through time, and what ramifying effects our behaviour may generate, can one hope to be effective in engineering change. This applies equally to being effective as a game participant, or when actually filling a managerial role in a real-life organisation.

References and notes

1   Stewart, W A C , *and* McCanny W P 'The Educational Innovators' Vol 2, '*Progressive Schools, 1881-1967*' (Macmillan, 1963)
2   Bligh, D A *What's the Use of Lectures* (Wiley, 1971)
3   The game format, originally introduced by Professor Goodman of Ann Arbor University, Michigan, has been considerably modified to

render it relevant to social services experience. The early work of modification was undertaken in co-operation with members of the Local Government Operational Research Unit. For other developments of the game see P Tansey *Educational Aspects of Simulations* (McGraw Hill 1971) and M W Monroe *Urban Games: Four Case Studies in Urban Development* (University of California 1972). Suppliers of relevant games are Urbex Affiliates Inc.

4 Role-players designations can be changed according to the objectives of the game and personnel concerned. If the primary aim is to train workers in field-level decisions, it would be possible to define roles in terms of a range of specialisms within social work. If the primary focus is on interdepartmental relations, the eight roles allocated might be those of chief executive, treasurer, director of establishments, chief education officer, director of social services, director of transport services, chief architect, chief amenities officer, chief planning officer.

5 Influence is defined as the power, capacity or other means available to motivate, direct, control, bias or otherwise gain ascendency for one's own values, objectives, or interests in a situation. Influence derives from a number of sources. It may result from formal authority or command over large resources; from personal contact with key decision-makers; from personal charisma; or from superior knowledge in a situation where this is recognised.

6 As with other aspects of the game, the greater the player's ability to predict changes in the system, the greater becomes his capacity to use his predictive knowledge in gaining his objectives. Though in real-life, this is normally a behaviour feature associated with prestige, the telescoped time period of the game requires that this is directly represented in variations in influence.

Appendices

Essential game materials]
This section contains all the materials necessary to play the game, with the exception of the scoreboards illustrated or referred to in the text. They are:

I CO-ORDINATOR'S BRIEFING NOTES A summary of the main elements of the game which the authors have used when briefing players before the game begins. On occasions it has paid dividends to brief the group in detail several days before the game is to be played, and to start the game day with only a short reminder of the complexities.

II BRIEFING NOTES FOR PLAYERS This is a much simplified version of the co-ordinator's notes which can be distributed to players before the day of the game.

III LIST OF AGENDA ITEMS This is the most important single piece of equipment for the game. Every role-player should receive one during the initial briefing session. Its use is described in detail in the text.

IV OBJECTIVES AT START OF PLAY Each role-player is asked to complete this form before play begins. It serves two purposes. First it provides a basis for later evaluation, and, second, it ensures that role-players become quickly conversant with the list of agenda items.

V SEQUENCE OF EVENTS BETWEEN ROUNDS The mechanics of the game are necessarily complex—the system being simulated is even more complex. This list provides a chronological account of the steps which need to be taken between each round. The whole process may be completed in about twenty minutes when those concerned become accustomed to the sequence.

VI SOME DE-BRIEFING TOPICS Co-ordinators of the game, after having played the game once or twice, will quickly learn the best ways of handling the de-briefing session. As a general principle, the best results are gained from leaving as much of the analysis and interpretation of events to players as possible. The co-ordinator should act as a resource person. However, it may help to pose a number of questions for players to discuss.

VII MAIN LESSONS The note on the main lessons to be learnt from the game is a guide to co-ordinators when trying to summarise the feedback comments of players during a de-briefing session.

VIII ROOM LAYOUT A large room is needed, with tables and chairs as indicated on the diagram (or, indeed, in any preferred arrangement). One or two blackboards should be available for use by the players themselves, and the co-ordinator.

27

IX   AGENDA ITEM INFLUENCES SCORE SHEET   The member of the *System* responsible for assessing agenda item influences uses one of these per round to note his decisions about how the passing or failing of the item under discussion will affect the influence rating of other items on the agenda. He works during the round, preparing two sets of decisions—one assuming the item is passed, the other assuming failure.

X   SCORER'S VOTING SHEET   One per round is used by the scorers to keep a record of role-player's voting on current and non-current agenda items. The current issue votes affect whether or not the item is passed. Non-current item votes are added to the agenda items influence board. (See Sequence of events between rounds.)

XI   GAME RECORD SHEETS   These provide a means by which the scorer can keep a record of play, including all voting decisions and rulings of members of the *System*. Such a record is useful later for analysis of how the game developed.

XII   PROFILE OF A SOCIAL SERVICES DEPARTMENT   It is sometimes useful to provide a profile of a department as background information on the basis of which role-players may make their decisions during the game.

I Co-ordinator's briefing notes

In essence the game is about balancing *systematic rational decision-making* and *power and influence* to reach a more desirable situation.

A number of secondary objectives include:

1 To simulate the decision-making processes of policy-making and planning in a social services department.
2 To examine the ways in which conflicting interests are represented in decision-making, and how conflict is accommodated, resolved or avoided.
3 To provide an abbreviated experience of the different strategies necessary to effect change, given the range of influences and constraints working in different directions in respect of any proposed change.
4 To elucidate the political and managerial processes by which priorities are, or may be, decided upon.

In summary

We are concerned with highlighting the political aspects of management, demonstrating the kinds of agencies which are created out of the conflict of opposing interests and the extent to which an understanding of the total system can help us to develop rational decision-making methods.

The mechanics of the game have been designed to simulate as simply as possible elements of reality in a social service department. For training purposes, the game is simplified to make it possible to play in a single day.

ESSENTIAL ELEMENTS

In terms of method it is a 'walking-around-the-room' type of game.

Pairs and groups of *role-players* enter a series of discussions, conflicts, coalitions and bargains.

Members of the *System* periodically report on the influence that players' actions have had on the social service system within which they are operating.

A range of *scoreboards* is constantly updated and provides a running commentary on the state of play as the game proceeds.

The *action* takes place within a simulated social service department setting. The nature of this organisation is left to players to make their own assumption—if it is of any help, a neutral 'setting' may be provided.

Course members are divided into two main groups—role-players and members of the *System*. Each will be considered in turn.

Role-players

Players are allocated between eight roles as follows:

1 director, social services department
2 assistant director, fieldwork services
3 assistant director, residential care

4 assistant director, planning and research

5 assistant director, domiciliary and day care

6 chief administrative officer

7 training officer

8 president, consumers association

In the process of bargaining over agency policies, each role-player represents the interests of his/her own section or areas of responsibility. If there is a large number of players, each role may be represented by 3 players to incorporate simulation of inter-sectional differences and discussions. Under these circumstances the responsibilities per role may be distributed as:

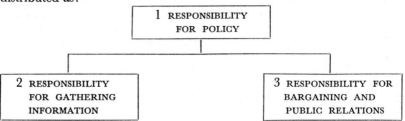

The eight roles refer simply to an expected or characteristic pattern of decision-making based on a combination of sectional interest and personal objectives.

Members of the System

Each represents particular features of the total system within which the role-players operate. They are *not* a simulated social service committee, but represent all the features of the system which are not simulated in some more specific way.

In addition there are:

2 scorers

1 or more observers

1 co-ordinator

MECHANICS

The game comprises a series of *rounds*. Usually 5 or 6 are played during a session. Each round involves the selection of an *agenda item* from the agenda item list. Role-players circulate and discuss the selected issue in the context of desired departmental policy, other items already passed or rejected, other items on the list, budgetary allowances, and other factors influencing the decision-making process. Having argued about the *current item* for 10-20 minutes *players vote, the issue passes or fails,* members of the *System* assess the affect of the passing or failing of that issue on the total system, and the process begins again.

Each player begins the game with a certain amount of *influence*. (Shown on *players influence board*.) Influence is simulated by *pegs*—2 pegs are allocated for each point of influence on the 12 point scale.

The pegs are used for voting on items of policy—ie the agenda items—as they arise during the course of the game.

As the game progresses the amount of influence of each player—ie the number of pegs he has available for voting—fluctuates according to the extent to which he or she succeeds in representing his or her own interests in the course of play. If a player succeeds, his voting power in the next round is increased, if he fails, it is reduced.

Throughout the game, players use their influence by voting on agenda items as they arise. Each role-player has a small *peg board* represented by a certain colour, and a number of pegs, which can be slotted into a range of alternative holes on the board to record votes.

Votes can be allotted in various ways:

1 *For* or *against* the current agenda item.
2 *For* or *against* one or more of the other agenda items on the list. This has the effect of promoting or demoting non-current issues and this influences their future likelihood of coming up for discussion and becoming part of departmental policy.
3 Influence can be *stored* against one of the external forces. [This simulates the tapping of the goodwill of parties outside the department in furthering intra-departmental objectives.] This stored influence may be retrieved at any time by the players and used in the normal way. Stored influence may be increased or decreased, however, depending on how these external bodies (simulated by the *System*) react to changes in departmental policy trends.

Players choose their voting strategy and vote according to their interests, but in the light of constraints such as the limited budget, the demands of fellow players for reciprocity and so on.

The *voting process* represents the decision-making procedure of the department on matters of policy. The outcome of the votes cast on each item, therefore, represents not only the acceptance or rejection of a particular agenda item detailed, but also the introduction of a specific direction or trend in department policy. Thus, for example, the passing of an item (no 10) to establish car allowances for home helps at an annual cost of £2,000 suggests the development of a policy extending community services.

Central to the play is the *list of agenda items*. The specific items included on the agenda reflect generalised issues covering the whole spectrum of different needs within a social services department. *They represent a wide range of alternative policies between which choices have to be made*, for example:

whether to develop community care services (item 10) or to extend or improve residential provision (item 11) or what balance to achieve between them and at what cost?

or preventive work (6) as opposed to improving social casualty services (25)?

31

or universalist services (29) versus selective services (30)?

No order of agenda items is laid down in advance of the game, but each has a prior degree of likelihood of coming up for discussion, (and thus of being passed) based on precedent, tradition and fashion. *This is expressed in terms of pegs pre-cast in favour of or against each issue on the agenda.* Every item is rated on a + 25 to − 25 point scale according to the amount of influence it commands within the system.

This rating is revised at the end of every round on the basis of:

1   decisions of the *System*

2   voting on non-current items

The initial influence positions at the start of the game are the final positions reached in the previous game, reversed to produce an initial disequilibrium.

SELECTION OF ISSUES FOR DISCUSSION AND VOTING

At the start of each round, one item is selected for discussion and voting. For this purpose a large bag of table tennis balls represents the element of chance at work. It contains:

1   *32 balls numbered* 1-32, each corresponding to an agenda item. Thus an item may arise through *chance* which no-one really wants to discuss.

2   *32 blank balls* If a blank is drawn, the issue with the greatest amount of existing influence comes up for discussion.

Thus there is a 50-50 chance of random, unpredictable factors altering the course of the planning process.

An item passes or fails as a result of voting at the end of each round

Added into the calculation is the *existing degree of influence* for that item. For example:

Example

$$
\begin{array}{ll}
+20 & \text{votes for} \\
-30 & \text{votes against} \\
+25 & \text{existing points of influence} \\
\hline
+15 &
\end{array}
$$

The item is passed despite a negative vote.

Note

A *passed* or *rejected* item, is replaced by another item (plus an estimate of the cost) proposed by the player with most influence after that round. At the start of the game each role-player is asked to complete a short questionnaire. This will provide a basis for personal evaluation after the game has been played.

The *System* articulates all those tangible and intangible factors and constraints of the total social service system in which the role-players operate which are not more specifically represented in the simulation. They calculate the effects of decisions. Their deliberations are based on their assessment of the effect on other parts of the system of the passing or failing of the current agenda item, discussed and voted on in the previous round.

The *System* answers the question: 'What sort of social service agency is being developed by the sum total of decisions made by the players, round by round?'

The work is performed by 4 or more players, each dealing with a particular aspect as follows:

1   Agenda item influences

This person (or persons) assesses the effect of the passing or failing of the current agenda item on each of the other items on the agenda. This is undertaken on the assumption that passage or failure of an item reflects extant departmental policy, and that other items associated with this policy increase or decrease in influence accordingly.

Thus the influence rating (on the $+25$ to -25 point scale) is reassessed for each item in the light of the most recent round of voting. [There are 2 main ways in which influence is affected: item A needs item B therefore B's influence increases; item A obviates need for B therefore B's influence is reduced.] Some items are only linked by virtue of the fact that they are in the same system competing for scarce resources, therefore very difficult choices have to be made.

After members of the *System* have announced the agenda item influence ratings, the score boards are changed and brought up-to-date.

2   Player influences

Members ask the question: 'What effect will the passing or rejection of this item have on the level of influence of each of the role-players?' This influence, rated on 12 point scale, is altered accordingly.

This influences the number of pegs, and thus the players' voting power, in the next round.

3   External influences

This member examines the effect of the passing or rejection of the current item on each of the external forces—MASS MEDIA, PRESSURE GROUPS, CENTRAL GOVERNMENT and PROFESSIONAL ASSOCIATIONS (ie player influence board rating $\times$ 2.

Influence is rated on a 1-10 point scale. This effects increases or decreases in the influence (ie number of influence pegs) stored by players under each of these headings.

4   Total structural influences

The fourth member of the *System* examines the total state of the boards, general trends in voting, trends and developments in departmental policy. In short, he summarises the state of play and highlights strengths and weaknesses.

At the end of each round, each member of the *System*

a gives general indication of the assumptions on which detailed changes have been made, and

b announces the detailed changes in levels of influence.

No decision of a member of the System *can be questioned.* Players must attempt to understand the *System's* logic and work on that understanding.

II Briefing notes for players

OBJECTIVES

In essence the game is about balancing systematic, rational decision-making and power and influence in the allocation of scarce resources within a social service department. It has a number of secondary objectives:
1   To simulate the decision-making processes of policy and planning in social service departments
2   To examine the ways in which conflicting interests are represented in decision-making, and how conflict is accommodated, resolved or avoided
3   To provide an abbreviated experience of the different strategies necessary to effect change, given the range of influences and constraints working in different directions in respect of any proposed change
4   To elucidate the political and managerial processes by which priorities are, or may be, decided upon.

In summary
We are concerned with highlighting the political aspects of management, demonstrating the kinds of agencies which are created out of the conflict of opposing interests and the extent to which an understanding of the work system can help us to develop more rational decision-making methods.

   The mechanics of the game have been designed to simulate as simply as possible elements of reality in a social service department. Each element in the game is *symbolic* of some part of reality.

ESSENTIAL ELEMENTS

It is a 'walking-around-the-room' type of game. Pairs and groups of role-players enter into a series of *discussions, negotiations* and *bargains*. *Periodic reports* are made (by the *System*) on the way the game is going. A range of scoreboards is constantly updated and provides a running commentary on the state of play as the game proceeds. The *action* takes place in a simulated social service department setting. (The nature of this organisation is left for role-players to make their own assumptions.)

Course members are divided into two main groups—role-players and members of the *System*. Each will be considered in turn.

Role-players
Players are allocated between 8 roles—7 members of a social service department plus one co-opted consumer representative.
   In the process of bargaining over agency policies, each role-player represents the interests of his/her own section or areas of responsibility.

Members of the System
Each represents a particular feature of the total system within which the role-players operate. They are *not* a simulated social service committee but represent all the features of the system which are not simulated in some more specific way.

35

In addition there are:

2 scorers

1 or more observers

1 co-ordinator

MECHANICS

The game comprises 5 or 6 *rounds*. At the beginning of each round an *agenda item* is selected from the agenda item list. Role-players circulate and discuss the selected issue in the context of desired departmental policy, other items already passed or rejected, other items on the list, budgetary allowances etc. Having argued the *current item* for 20 minutes the role-players *vote*, the issue passes or fails, and members of the *System* assess the affect of the passing or failing of that issue on the total system and the whole process begins again.

INFLUENCE AND VOTING

Each player begins the game with a certain amount of *influence*. Influence is simulated by *pegs*—2 pegs for each point of influence shown on the *players influence board*. Influence pegs are used for voting on items of policy during the game.

As the game progresses the influence of each player ie the number of pegs available for voting, varies according to the extent to which he/she succeeds in representing his/her sectional interests.

At the end of each round players use their influence pegs to vote on agenda issues. Each role-player has a small peg-board on which to record his votes.

Votes can be allotted in 3 ways:

1 *For* or *against* the current agenda item.

2 *For* or *against* one or more of the other agenda items on the list. (This increases or decreases the likelihood of non-current issues coming up for discussion).

3 Influence can be stored against one of the external forces—a kind of investment in the goodwill of the mass media, pressure groups, central government or professional associations. Stored influence can be retrieved at any time and used in the normal way. It may increase or decrease depending on how these parties react during the game to developments in departmental policy.

The *voting process* represents the decision-making procedure of the department on matters of policy. Individual issues passed and rejected represent directions or trends in that policy.

The order of agenda items is not predetermined, although each has a prior degree of likelihood of being discussed (and thus of being passed) based on precedent, tradition and fashion. This is expressed in terms of pegs pre-cast in favour of or against each item on the agenda, on a +25 to −25 point scale. This rating is revised at the end of every round on the basis of:

1 *System* decisions and

2 Voting

Items are selected at the beginning of every round. A large bag contains 64 table tennis balls—32 are numbered 1-32; 32 are blank. If a numbered ball is drawn that item is discussed (representing the element of chance). If a blank ball is drawn, the item discussed is that with the highest influence rating on the *agenda items board*.

An item passes or fails as a result of the voting during that round.

Added or substracted to the votes cast by role-players is the *existing level of influence* which that item commands.

THE SYSTEM

Members of the *System* articulate all the intangible factors and constraints within the system not otherwise simulated. They calculate and report on the effects of decisions during play. Their deliberations are based on an assessment of the effect on other parts of the system of the passing or failing of the current agenda item voted on in the previous round.

Four aspects are identified:

1 *Agenda item influences*

The effect on all other agenda items of the voting in the last round is assessed, and the influence of each of these items is altered accordingly.

2 *Player influences*

'What effect will the passing or failing of this item have on the influence-rating of each of the role-players?' Players' ratings on the 12 point scale are altered accordingly—thus increasing or reducing players' voting power in subsequent rounds.

3 *External influences*

The effect of passing or failing of items on each of the external bodies is examined, and ratings changed accordingly on a 10 point scale.

4 *Total structural influences*

Each member of the *System*:

a gives a general indication of the assumptions on which detailed changes have been made and

b itemises all changes to the influence ratings.

No decision of a member of the System *can be questioned.* Players must attempt to understand the logic and work on that understanding.

Passed or rejected items are replaced by an issue (plus an estimate of the cost) proposed by the player with most influence at the end of that round.

III Agenda items

*Estimated additional
annual cost in £'s*

1	Establish a project team with full power of implementation to investigate and improve record keeping throughout the agency	3,000
2	Relocate all neighbourhood offices in various priority areas of need	24,000
3	Modernise all the agency's offices and provide proper interviewing rooms in each neighbourhood centre	20,000
4	Increase the secretarial staff	24,000
5	Set up a scheme for recruiting, training and using voluntary workers	2,000
6	Set up pre-school play-groups in 2 areas of high need	12,500
7	Increase use of funds available for expenditure on children's upkeep over the next year	5,000
8	Increase foster-parent boarding out allowances	60,000
9	Pay a grant to keep the local family planning clinic in existence which health department has turned down	1,200
10	Establish allowance for cars for home helps	2,000
11	Establish a career ladder for residential staff	1,000
12	Increase number of residential placements for maladjusted children	3,000
13	Produce a report on need for a drug addiction clinic for the chief medical officer	500
14	Establish sufficient sheltered workshops for those not able to work in open employment (capital cost—£120,000)	6,000
15	Second 10 fieldworkers for intensive groupwork and community work training over the next 2 years	5,000
16	Establish a post of social work liaison officer with housing department	1,500
17	Double the number of sheltered housing facilities	15,000
18	Establish two joint social work appointments with the two local hospitals	3,000
19	Establish group homes for the employable mentally ill	1,000
20	Set up a residential home for those physically handicapped not requiring hospital treatment (capital cost—£150,000)	36,000
21	Establish social workers in 10 general practices as a pilot experiment	15,000
22	Decentralise administration under area officers	24,000
23	Set up a working party with architects, treasurers and management services (work study specialists) to design model cost-effective homes for each different type of client need	4,000
24	Allot two places to client representatives on the social services committee	0

25	Appoint a skilled psychodynamically-oriented case-worker to the training officer team	4,000
26	Call in operational research consultants to predict amount of future needs which social services might be trying to meet	5,000
27	Establish a post of social planner	5,600
28	Establish 'market stall' information centres at strategic positions throughout the area	2,000
29	Produce a welfare rights booklet to be distributed to every household in the area	1,000
30	Set up a rehabilitation unit for homeless families	80,000
31	Build one modern purpose built old people's home (capital cost—£80,000)	8,000
32	Open small modern hostel for mentally ill with full day care facilities	60,000

Total potential expenditure £434,300

Budget allocation=£143,800 (ie 33 per cent of Total)

IV Objectives at start of play

ROLE:

Write a brief statement of the policies you would like to see the department pursue during the course of the game.

List in order of importance the six most important agenda items in pursuing this policy.

1

2

3

4

5

6

List the six agenda items which would be most likely to negate your policy objectives.

1

2

3

4

5

6

List a further six agenda items of your own choosing which would promote your policy objectives.

1

2

3

4

5

6

V Sequence of events between rounds

1 Time called—players boards returned to desk.
2 Transfer *stored* influence pegs to external influences board.
3 General comments from *System* members about the assumptions on which their judgements have been based.
4 Votes for and against current agenda item counted number of pegs x 2). Voting on current item + existing level of influence=result
5 Announcement of voting and result.
6 Add points for and against other agenda items on score sheet.

Reports from members of the System.

7 Agenda items: information on new position of agenda items; results of deliberations during round on the basis; of possible results from vote on current item; statement of new positions and basic trends Agenda item boards altered by scorer accordingly (and record kept).
8 Players influence—information on new role-player influence levels and justifications.
Player influence board altered accordingly by scorer (and record kept). Prepare players boards for next round. Number of pegs to be put on players boards is their influence rating x 2.
9 External forces—report on effect of new position of agenda items on each of external agents, scored on a 10 point scale. External forces score noted on scoreboard (and record kept by scorer). Stored influence pegs are altered accordingly. For example:
3 pegs or less = −1 or +1 for any change; more than 3 pegs = flat rate levy or addition according to the direction of movement on 10 point scale.
10 Total structural influences—assessment of general policy and trends
11 Change position of pegs on agenda item boards as a result of voting scores (from score sheet).
12 New agenda item chosen by selecting a ping pong ball from the bag:
if number drawn has already been played, there will be another item in its place, chosen from co-ordinator's list, or from player's list;
if blank is drawn, the agenda item with most existing support is played. If there is more than one item with the same existing support, the player with the most influence chooses one from them.

VI Some de-briefing topics

Progress of game

1 What aspects of the game did/did not reflect reality? How could the game be modified to better simulate a department of this kind? What changes would make it more realistic?

2 Is it possible to identify any particular phases of development within the game? Identify, explain what and why.

3 What were the key elements which determined the course of play?

Role players, strategies and tactics

4 How did the various role-players play their roles? What leadership styles emerged? What types of power and authority emerged?

5 What strategies and tactics were employed by which role players to effect change? What part was played by reciprocity, fear, machiavellian manoeuvring, compromise, concession, power and influence, direction etc? What strategies and tactics proved most/least effective?

6 How were decisions made about which role-players to approach for support on the various issues?

7 Did players remain within the rules as outlined? Where was it necessary to break or bend the rules? Was this the only tactic? Was this realistic? Why did no-one break the rules and change the system in a radical way?

8 What groups and alliances were formed? How? Around what issues?

9 How were constraints/opposition/external disruptions dealt with?

10 What was the effect of newspaper/government announcements during the course of play?

Issues

11 How (if at all) were priorities between issues established?

12 Was the simulated relationship between agenda issues realistic?

Gaming

13 Has the game simulation technique any value (and if so what) in training, removing inhibitions, providing a tool for inter-agency co-operation, policy-maker?

14 Could a similar game be usefully employed, and with what effect, in a real local authority social services department?

Summary

15 What are the main lessons from the game?

VII Main lessons

1 Various alternative approaches to decision-making about action and priorities may be viable depending on the circumstances (eg incrementalism or rationalism). Planning is vital if everyday work is to be effectively carried out.

2 Decision-making is not an entirely rational process of assessing advantages and disadvantages of alternative courses of action, but takes place within a socio-economic and political context. It is vital to be fully aware of interaction between human relations and systematic analysis aspects of decision-making to ensure a viable balance between them.

3 It is necessary to understand something of how the system operates before effective action for change can be taken within it.

4 It is important to identify, thence to modify, avoid or counteract the constraints on any desired course of action. It is possible to some degree to predict constraints on action and take steps to respond to them *before* action is taken to produce a change.

5 A wide variety of strategies and tactics may be employed to achieve desired changes.

6 Compromise, persuasion, discussion, presentation of 'cases' have a role in achieving change.

7 The relationship between individual action and co-ordinated attempts to achieve change is usually a complex one, but invariably requires careful handling.

8 Various group decision-making processes may be used, depending on the subject-matter of discussion.

9 Timing is a significant factor in presenting arguments and pressing for a particular desired change.

10 The relative importance of structure and personality in making decisions varies according to the situation.

11 The game simulates reality of behaviour and work at three levels:

a interpersonal relations and group interactions:

b actual reality of working in senior management group of a local authority;

c through mechanics and complexities of the game itself.

12 No matter how much research is carried out nor how many predictions are made, there is never one hundred per cent certainty that the decision taken will have the desired effect. Given the vulnerability of the decision-maker, how can he prepare contingency plans to cope with emergencies?

VIII Room layout

NOTES ON ROOM LAYOUT

1   Members of the *System* should be to some extent isolated from the bustle of the play, and must not be approached by role-players.

2   The score-boards should be on view to role-players at all times, but also need to be easily accessible to the scorers, the co-ordinator and, if necessary, to members of the *System*.

3   One should remember that at the end of each round role-players will be returning their voting boards to the scorer's desk. This, therefore, needs to be easily accessible. In addition, whilst the scorers are making their rapid calculations, members of the *System* are announcing their assumptions about trends to the assembled role-players. The scorer's desk should not, therefore, impede role players view or hearing of the *System* members.

4   The blackboards are used to provide information to role-players during the course of play. Blackboard 1 can be used to provide basic reminders to role players about game mechanics, such as the length of rounds, numbers of issues already passed, Blackboard 2 is used by the co-ordinator to inject into the game information about the environment within which the simulated social services department operates. This includes prepared news items, departmental circulars, local authority bulletins, and so on. Role-players may also choose to use the board to simulate a departmental newsletter.

5   Role-players may move the furniture around in any way they wish during the course of play. The room is initially arranged in this fairly 'neutral' way to avoid predetermining the way the game develops. If, for example the room is laid out with a large central table surrounded by chairs, role-players quickly form a 'meeting' around this table and tend to proceed as a group. As the desirability of some method of corporate planning is a major lesson of the game, to engineer this result early on by a suggestive room layout, is not desirable. It is far better to allow the role-players to develop this strategy (and re-arrange the furniture accordingly) during the course of play.

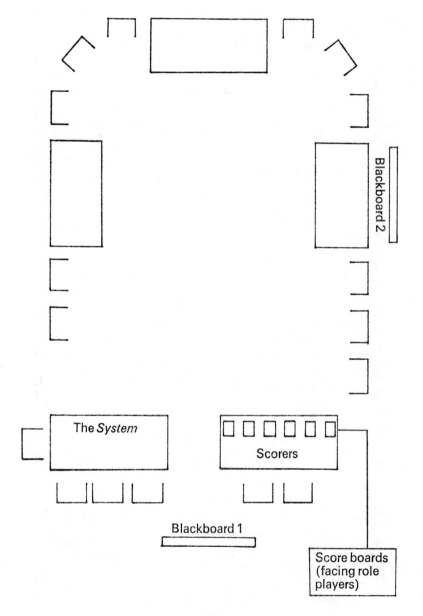

Blackboard 2

The *System*

Scorers

Blackboard 1

Score boards
(facing role
players)

IX Agenda item influences score sheet

Round [ ]

Agenda item	For					0	Against					Total
	+25	+20	+15	+10	+5	0	-5	-10	-15	-20	-25	
Current item												
1												
2												
3												
4												
5												
6												
7												
8												
9												
10												
11												
12												
13												
14												
15												
16												
17												
18												
19												
20												
21												
22												
23												
24												
25												
26												
27												
28												
29												
30												
31												
32												

X Scorer's voting sheet

Round [ ]

Agenda item	For								Against								Total
	1	2	3	4	5	6	7	8	1	2	3	4	5	6	7	8	
Current item																	
1																	
2																	
3																	
4																	
5																	
6																	
7																	
8																	
9																	
10																	
11																	
12																	
13																	
14																	
15																	
16																	
17																	
18																	
19																	
20																	
21																	
22																	
23																	
24																	
25																	
26																	
27																	
28																	
29																	
30																	
31																	
32																	

XI Game record sheet

a Agenda item influences

Agenda items Current item	1	2	3	4	5	6	7	8	9	10	11	12	13	14	15	16	17	18	19	20	21	22	23	24	25	26	27	28	29	30	31	32
start position																																
1																																
2																																
3																																
4																																
5																																
6																																

ROUNDS

48

b Player influence

start position	1 Director	2 Assistant Director, Fieldwork	3 Assistant Director, Residential Care	4 Assistant Director, Domiciliary and Day Care	5 Assistant Director, Planning and Research	6 Chief Administrative Officer	7 Training Officer	8 Consumer Representative
ROUNDS 1								
2								
3								
4								
5								
6								

49

c External forces

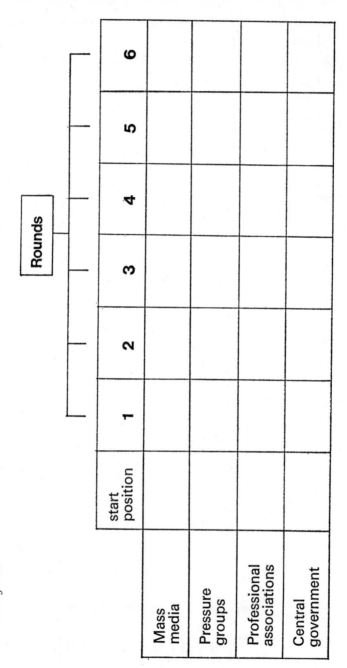

	start position	Rounds					
		1	2	3	4	5	6
Mass media							
Pressure groups							
Professional associations							
Central government							

d   Summary of results

Round no	Item no	Votes (net)	+ −	Existing influence	=	Result
1						
2						
3						
4						
5						
6						

XII Profile of a department

Borough
(An Inner London Borough with a population of 300,000)

Income - Expenditure Balance 1970/71

INCOME

	£
Rates	9,350,000
Rate equalisation	1,650,000
Government rate support grant	6,000,000
	17,000,000

EXPENDITURE

Borough Revenue expenditure (before payment of government grants)	10,500,000
Greater London Council	5,520,000
Metropolitan Police	980,000
	17,000,000

REVENUE EXPENDITURE

Social services	2,800,000
Highways and public works	2,400,000
Amenities	1,600,000
Housing	1,500,000
Health	1,000,000
Finance and general purposes	525,000
Planning and development	275,000
Miscellaneous	400,000
	10,500,000

PROPOSED CAPITAL EXPENDITURE OVER 5 YEAR PERIOD

Housing	8,000,000
Finance and general purposes	1,800,000
Highways and public works	850,000
Social services	500,000
Amenities	475,000
Planning and development	550,000
Health	130,000
Miscellaneous	395,000
	12,700,000

GLC EXPENDITURE

Education	3,500,000
Town planning and miscellaneous	850,000
Drainage	325,000
Fire services	260,000
Roads	250,000
Housing	210,000
Refuse disposal	125,000
	5,520,000

Borough

Social Services Department

Expenditure Summary 1970/71

		£
1	ADMINISTRATION	680,000

2 CHILDREN
In care:

Boarding out	65,000
Homes in borough	255,000
Homes not in borough	360,000
Other local authority and voluntary homes	42,000

Not in care:

Adoption	250
Family advice, youth and group work	55,000
Adventure playgrounds	23,000
Assistance in cash and kind	10,000
Day care of children	200,000
Miscellaneous	1,500

3 ELDERLY AND HANDICAPPED
Domiciliary Services:

Blind and handicapped	12,000
Elderly	40,000

Day centres:

Social and rehabilitation centres for blind and handicapped	20,000
Recreational and social centres for the elderly	16,000
Workshops for the elderly	22,000
Sheltered workshops and blind homeworkers	32,000

Residential accommodation:

Westbridge home for the retired	325,000
Other local authority and voluntary homes	140,000

Meals service:

Domiciliary and clubs	75,000

4 MENTAL HEALTH SERVICES

Training centres	43,000
Day centres	28,000
Residential accommodation	40,000
General miscellaneous	18,000

5 GENERAL SERVICES
Home helps   145,0000
Homeless families   150,000
Holiday homes   3,000
                                                 ─────────
                                    TOTAL 2,800,750
                                                 ─────────

Borough

Miscellaneous Statistics

	Borough	Average London (where applic.)
Population	300,000	
Density of population per acre	50.1	19.59
Product of penny rate	£50,500	
NO OF CHILDREN IN CARE		
% boarded out	25%	30%
% in local authority homes	45%	34%
% in voluntary homes and other	22%	26%
% in non-residential accommodation	8%	10%
No of children in care per 1,000 of population	3.3	2.0
No in care per 1,000 of population under 18 years	12.5	8.0
WELFARE		
% of population over 65	14%	12.4%
Homes for under 30 persons (2)—average number of residents	50	
Homes for over 50 persons (5)—average number of residents	900	
Homes for mentally ill (1)—number of places	60	
NO OF DISABLED PERSONS ON REGISTER (1969)		
Blind/Partially sighted/Defective sight		560
Physically handicapped		1,860
Deaf/Deaf and dumb/Hard of hearing		160